KRIS VAN DESSEL

SAMPLED HISTORY

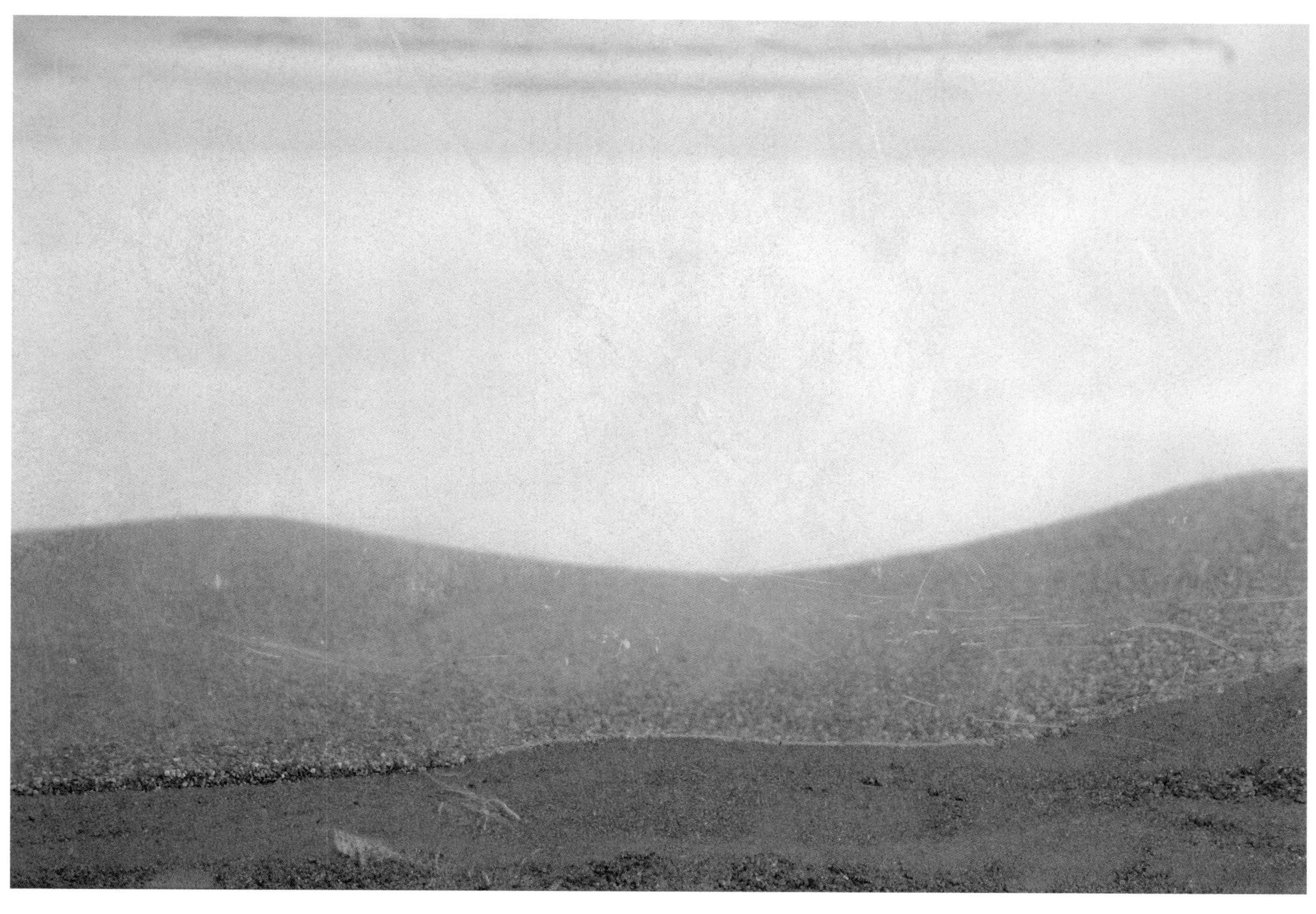

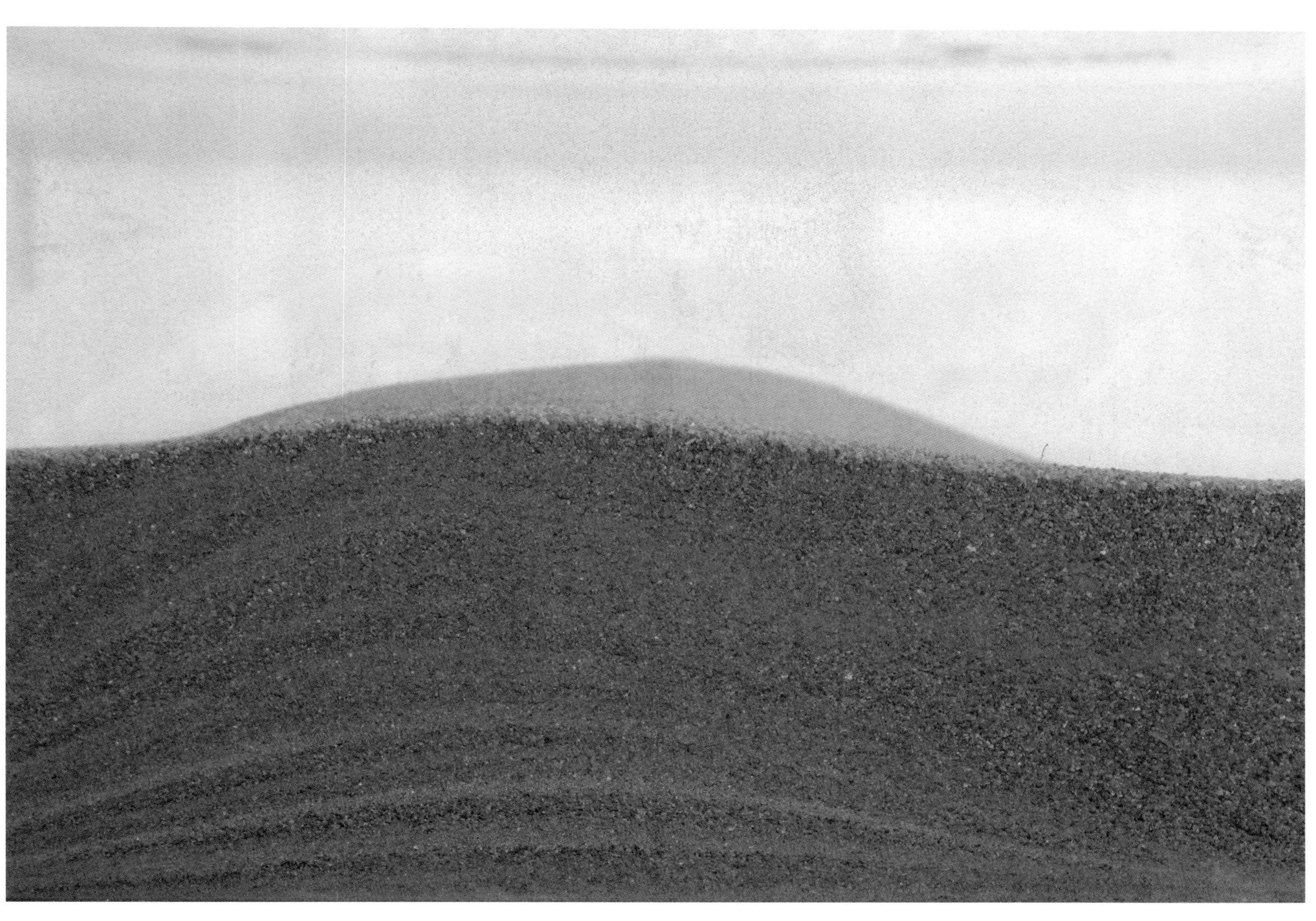

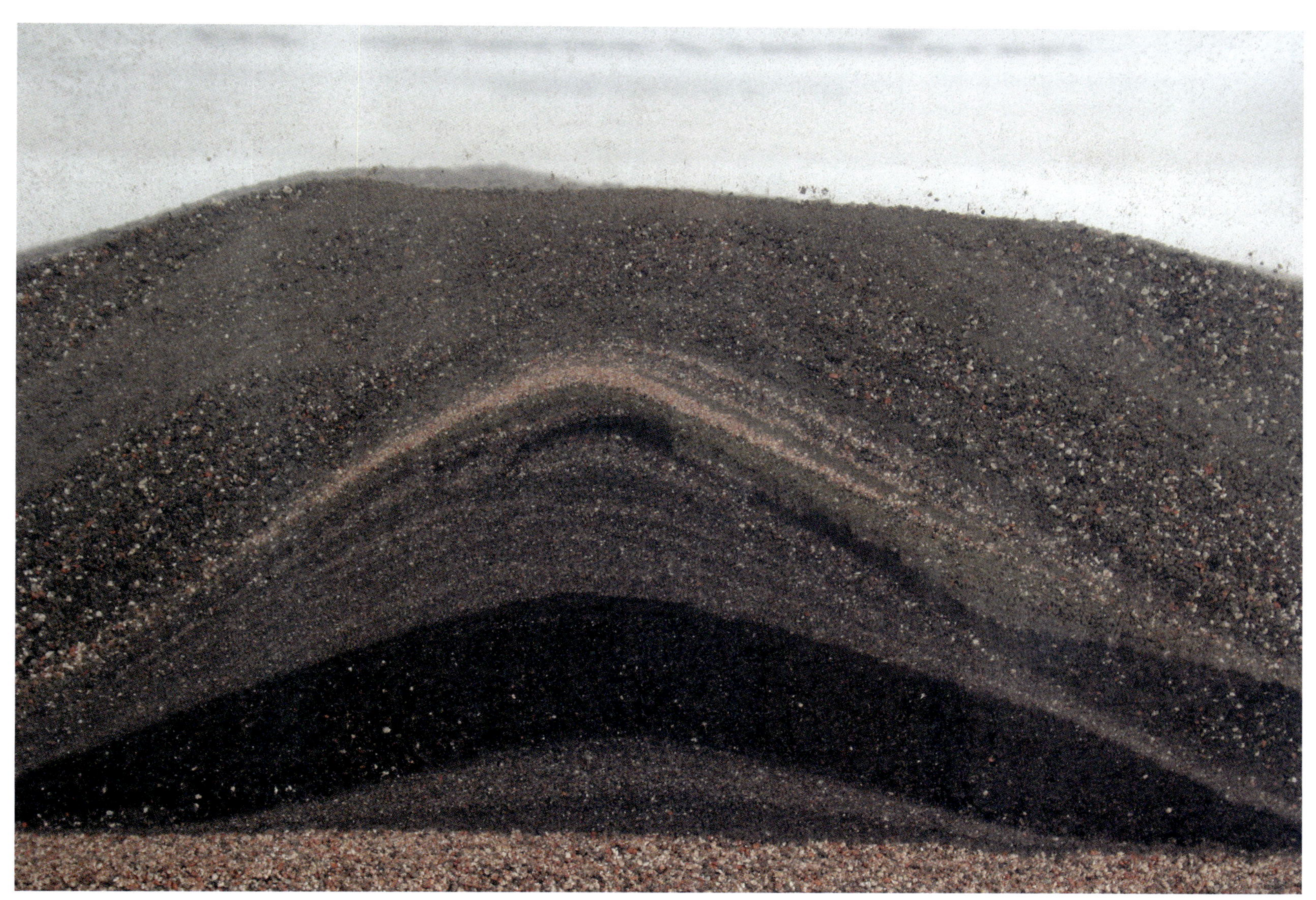

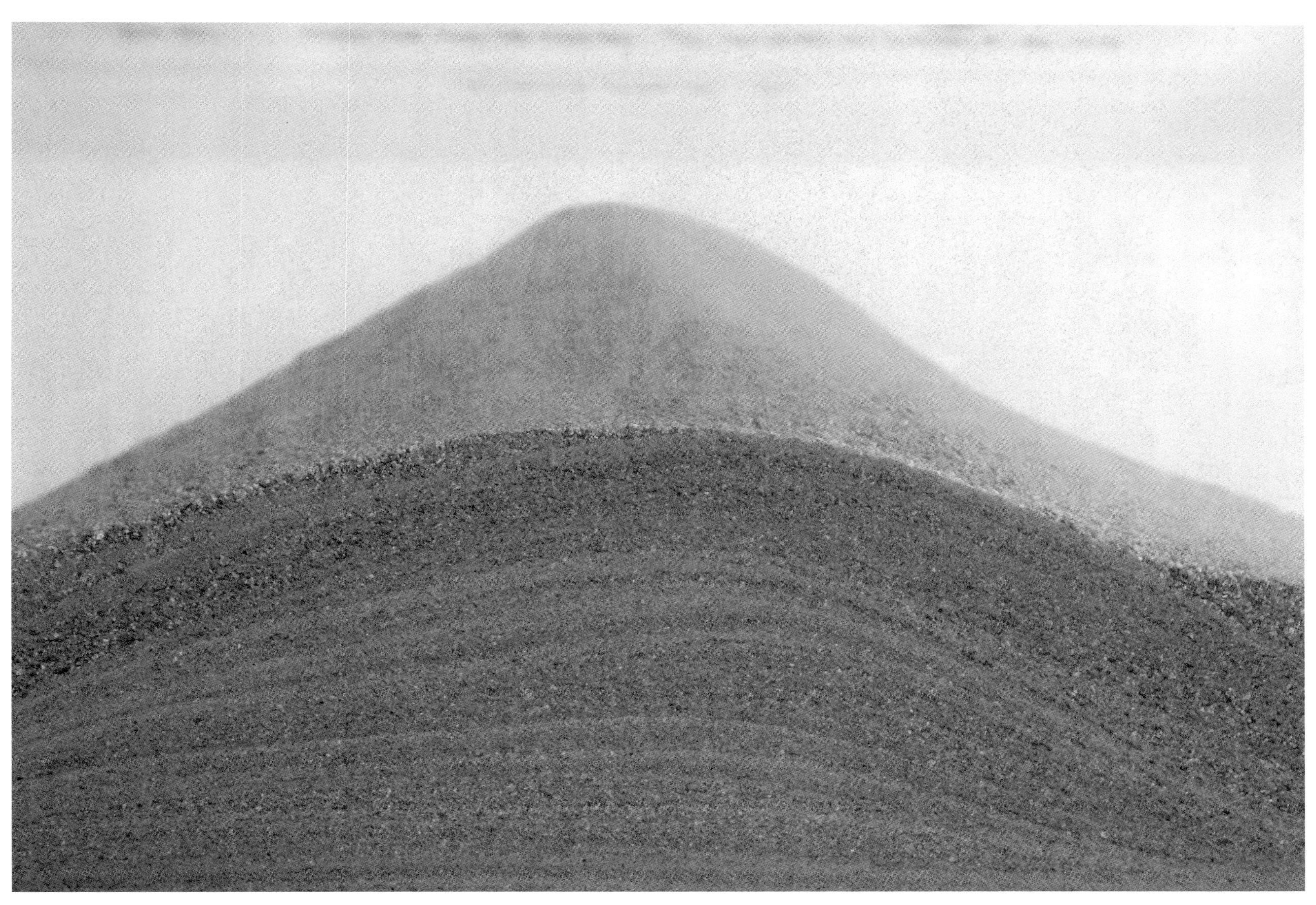

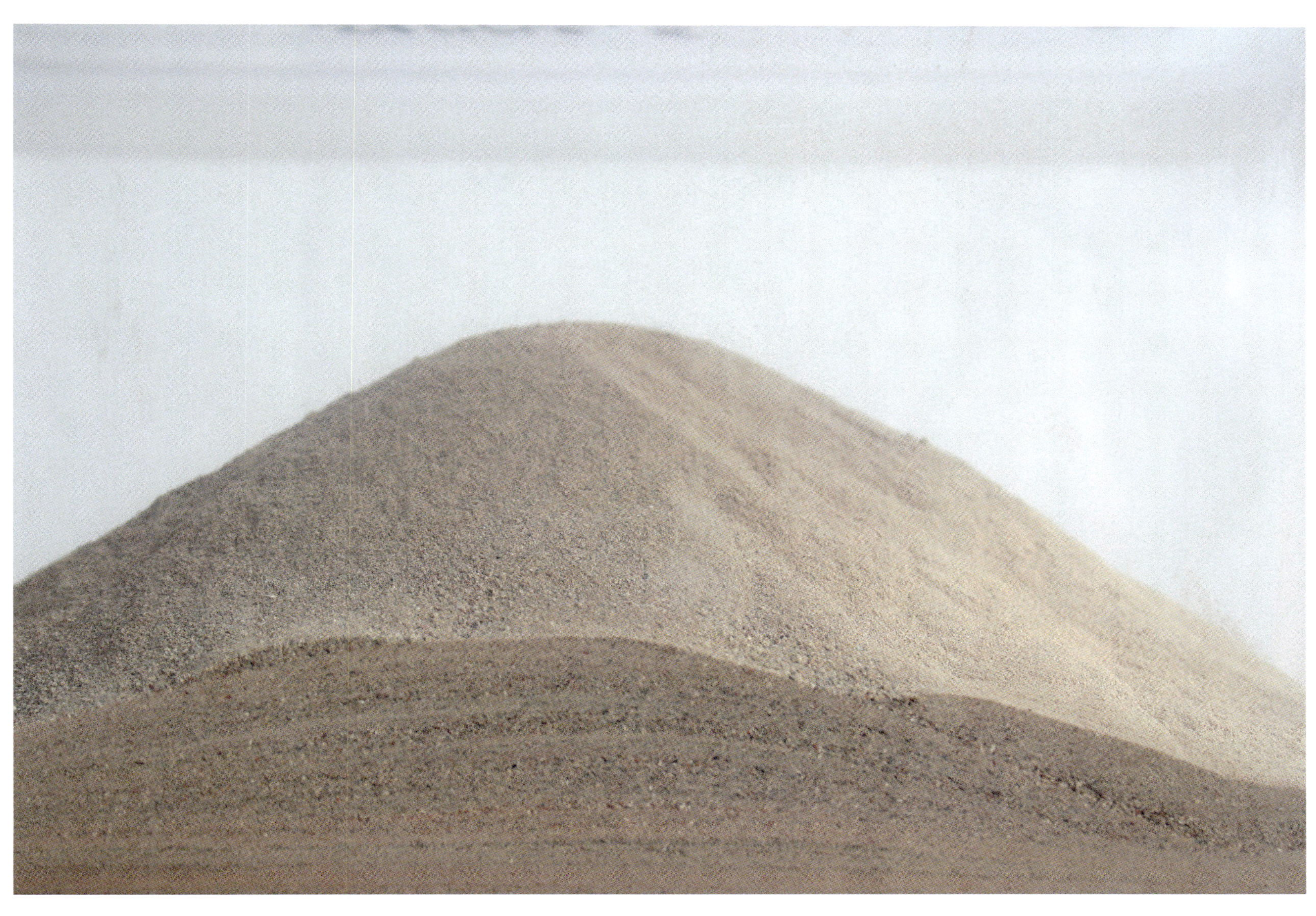

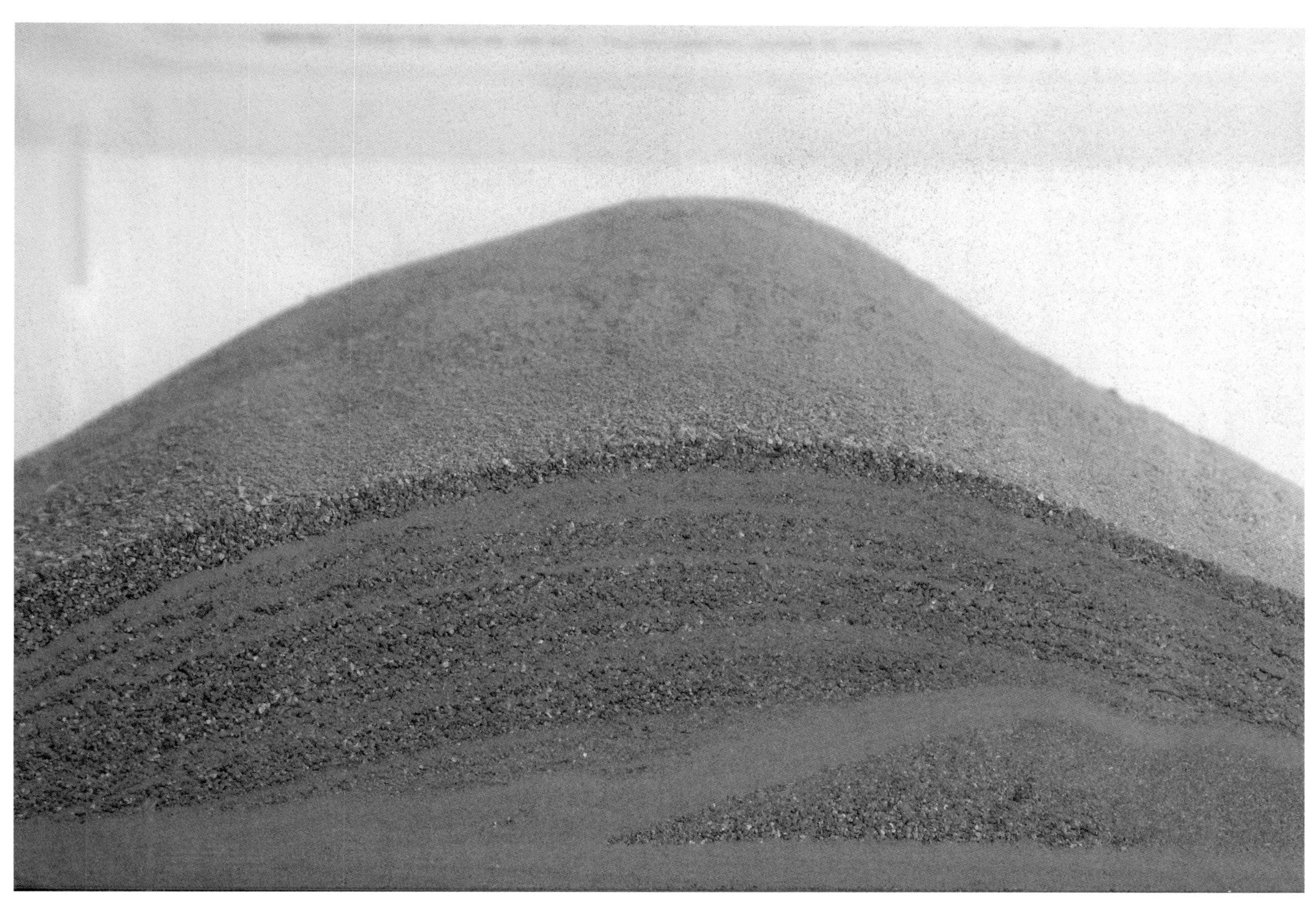

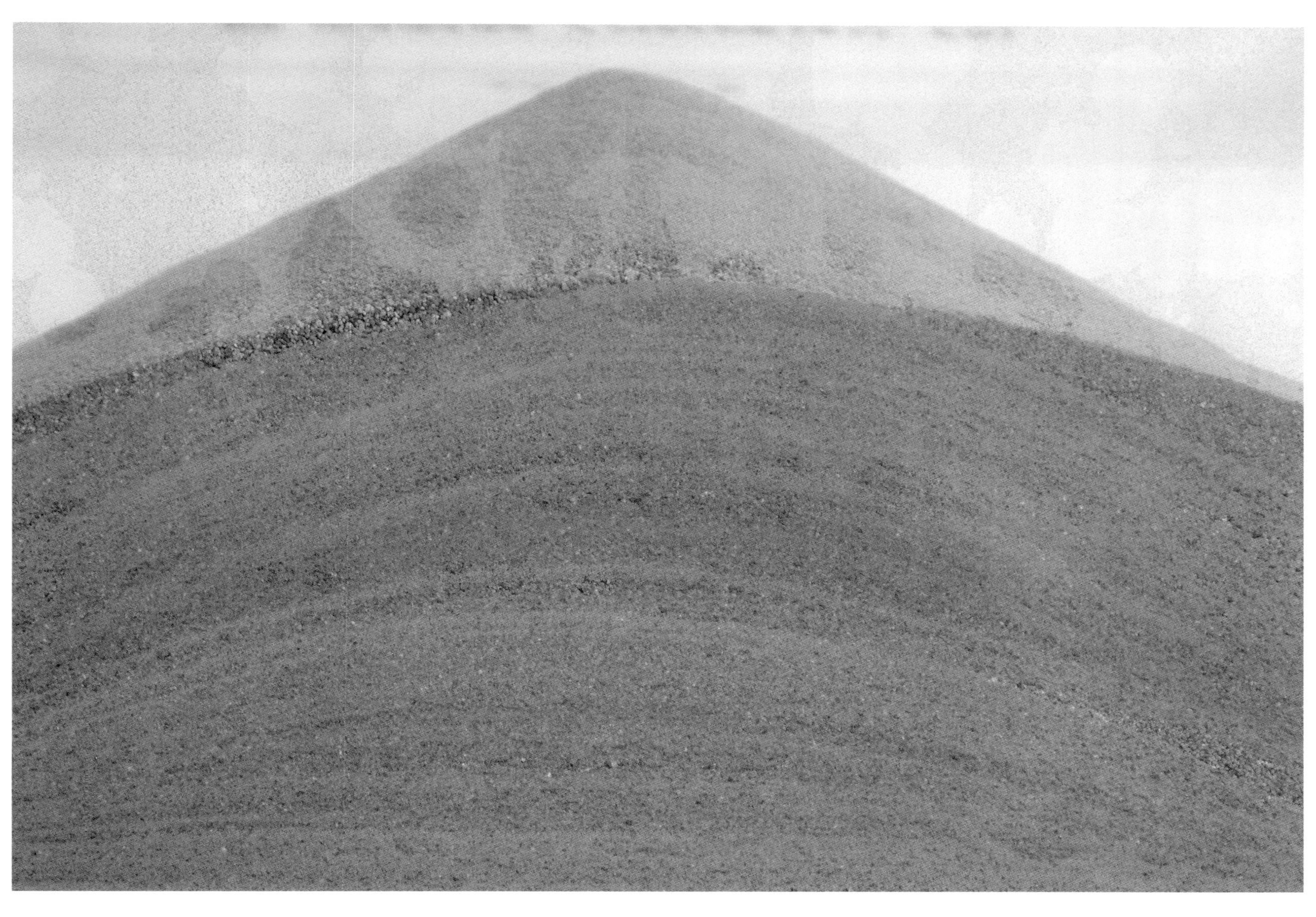

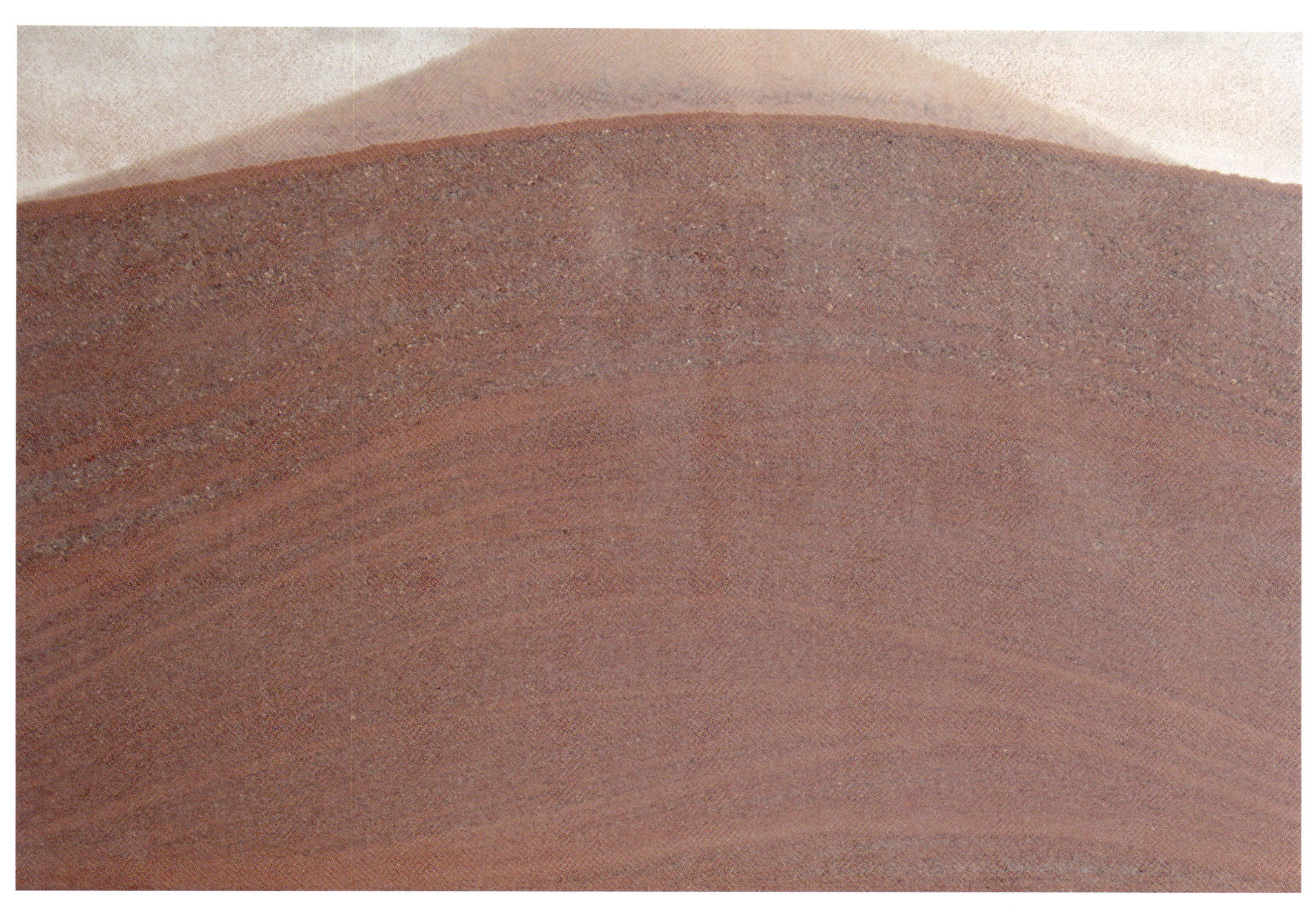

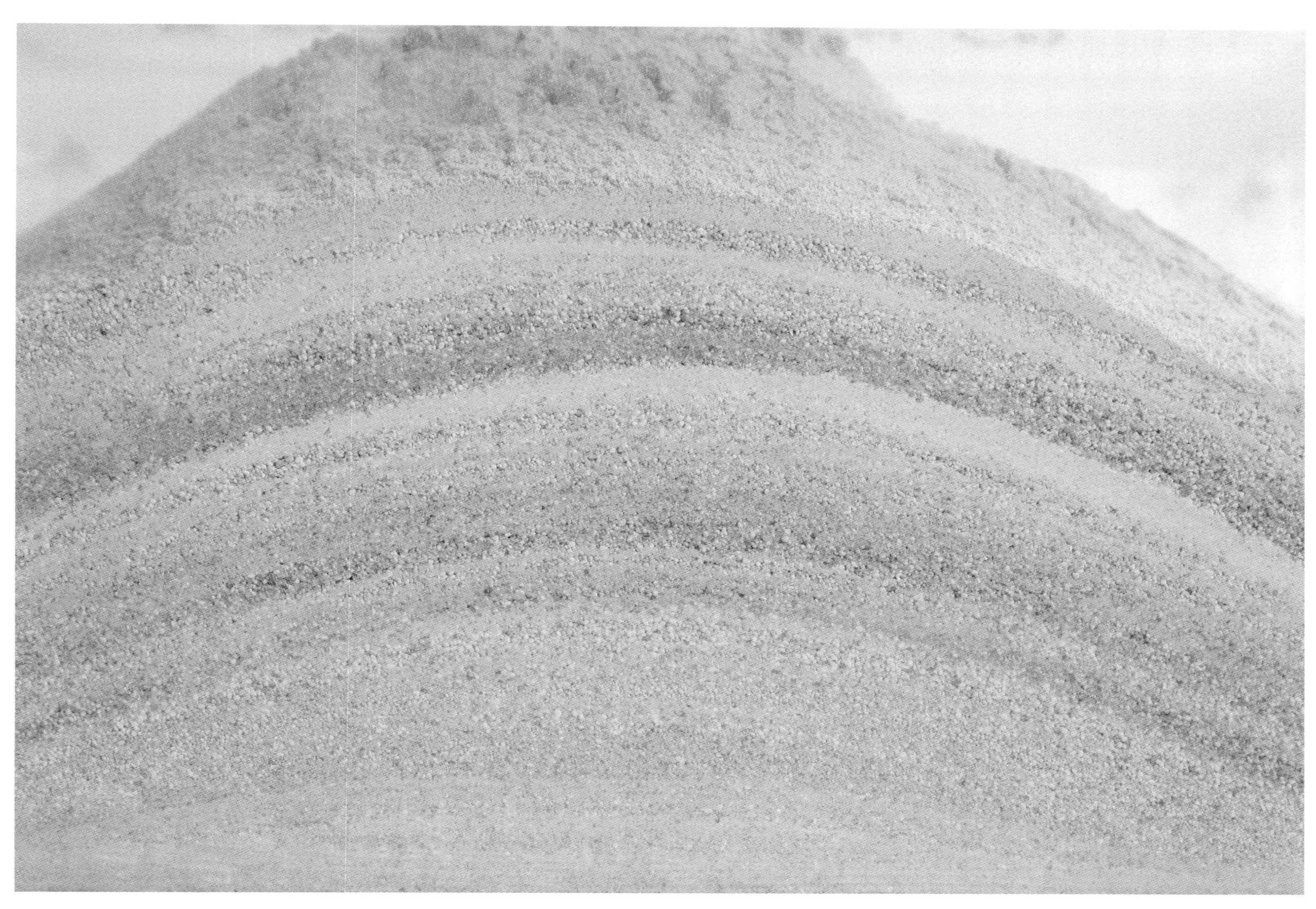

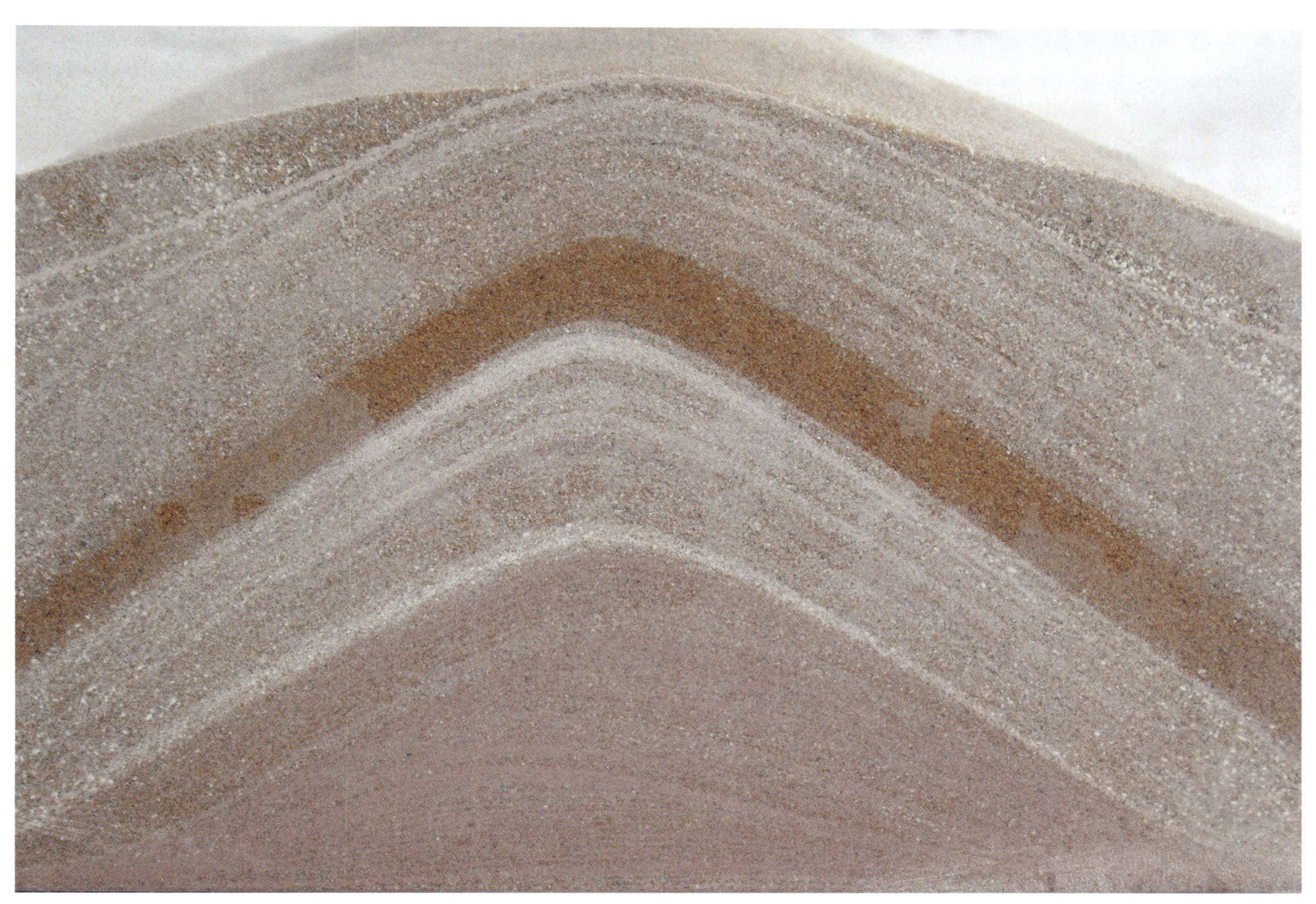

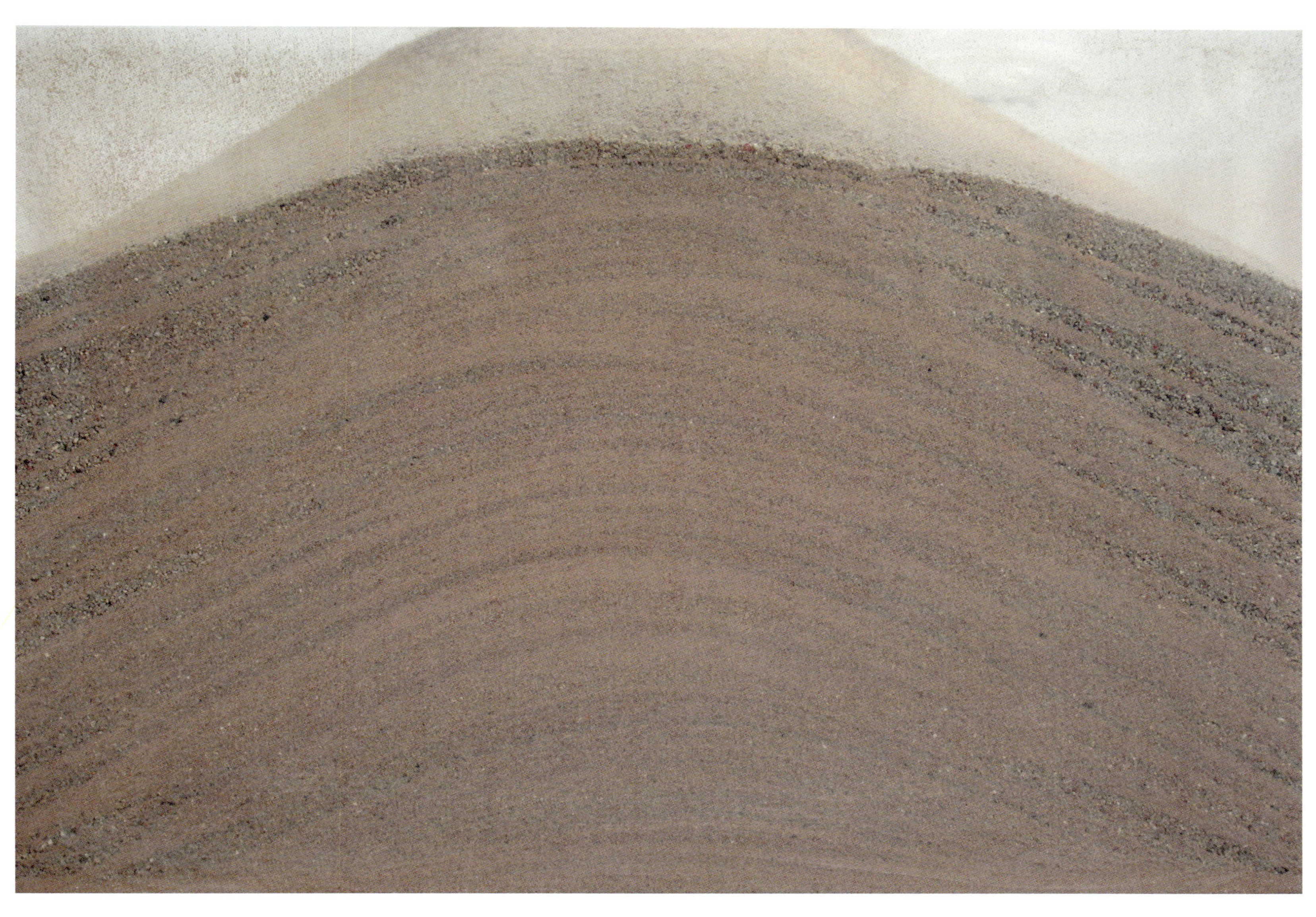

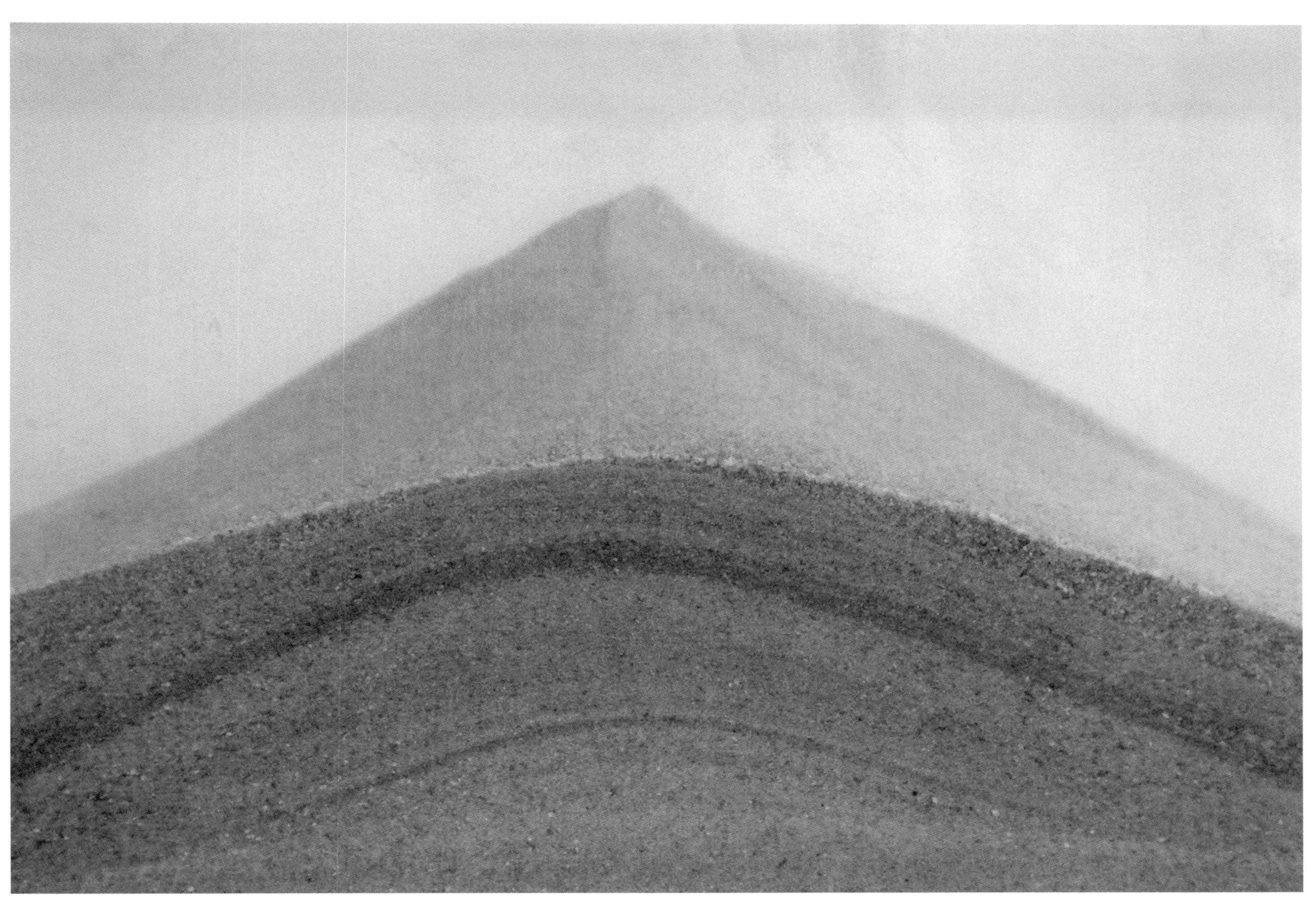

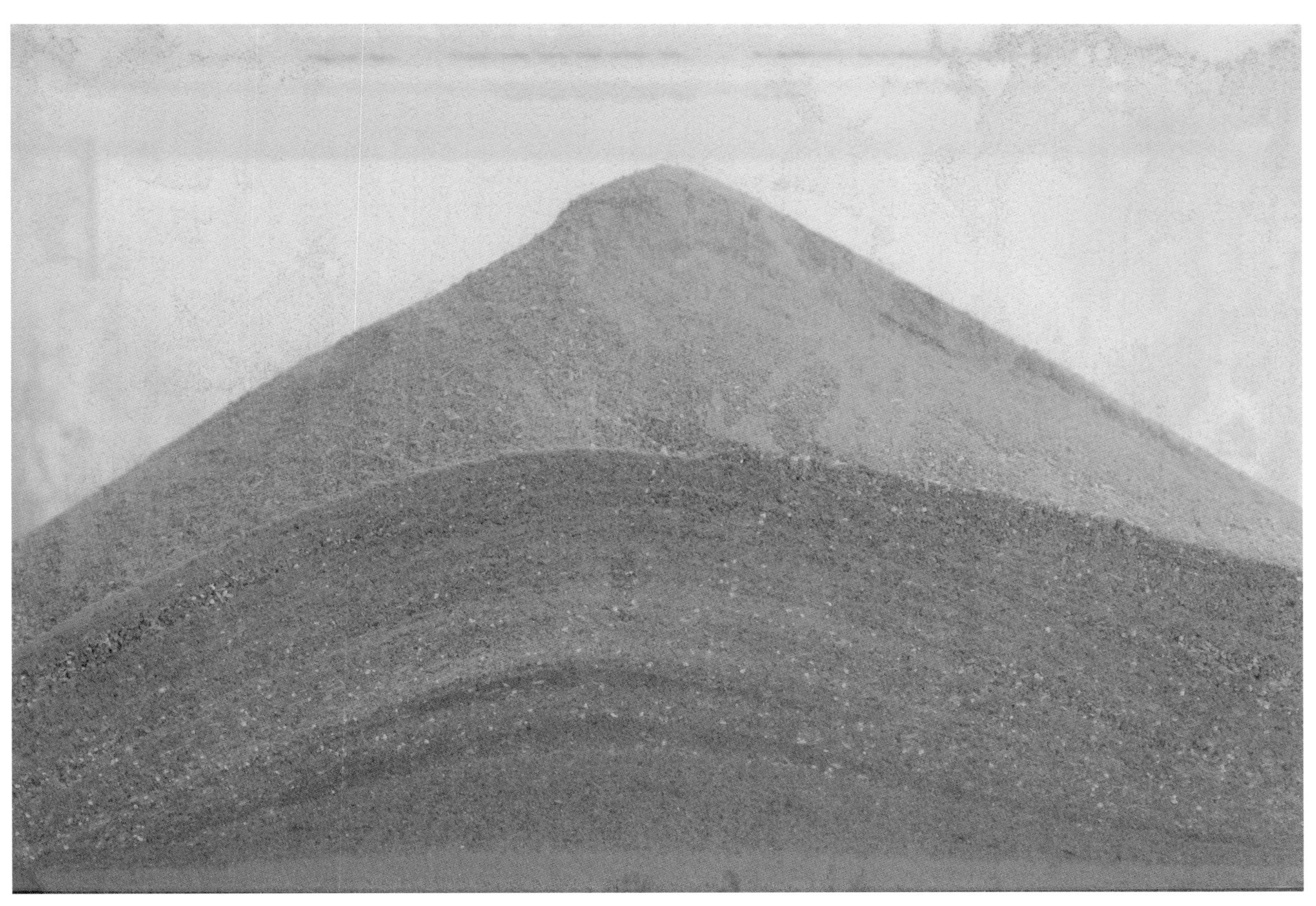

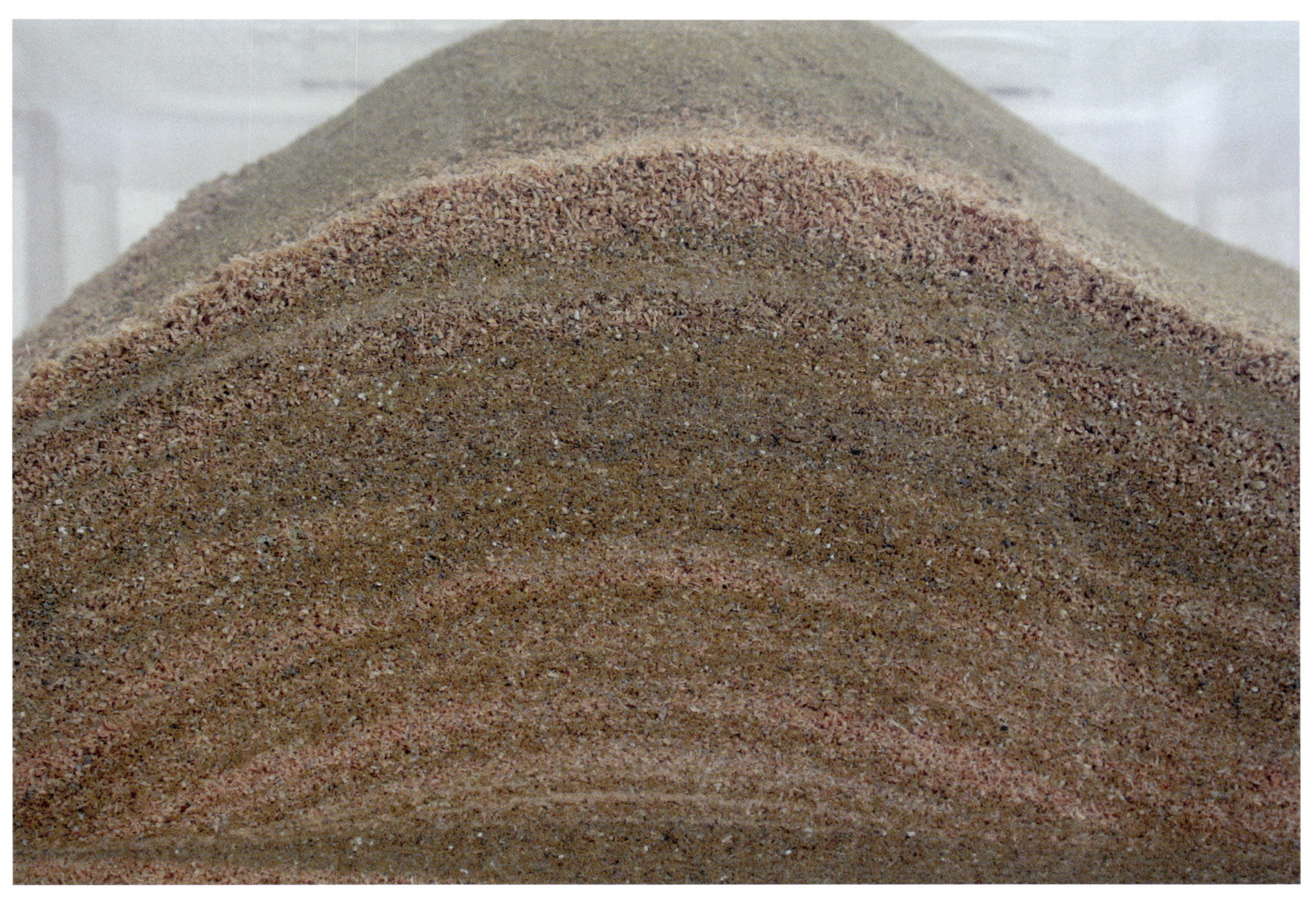

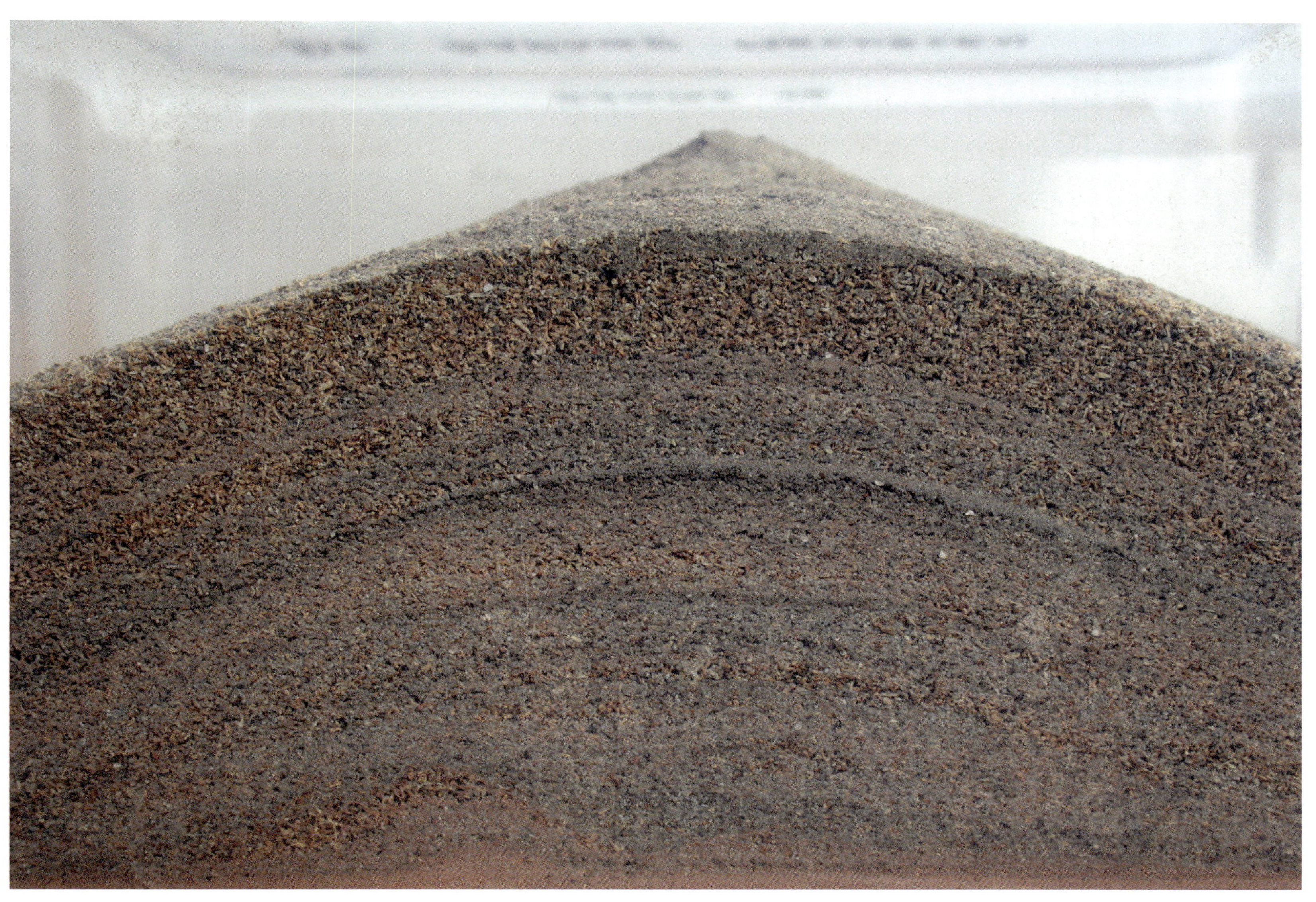

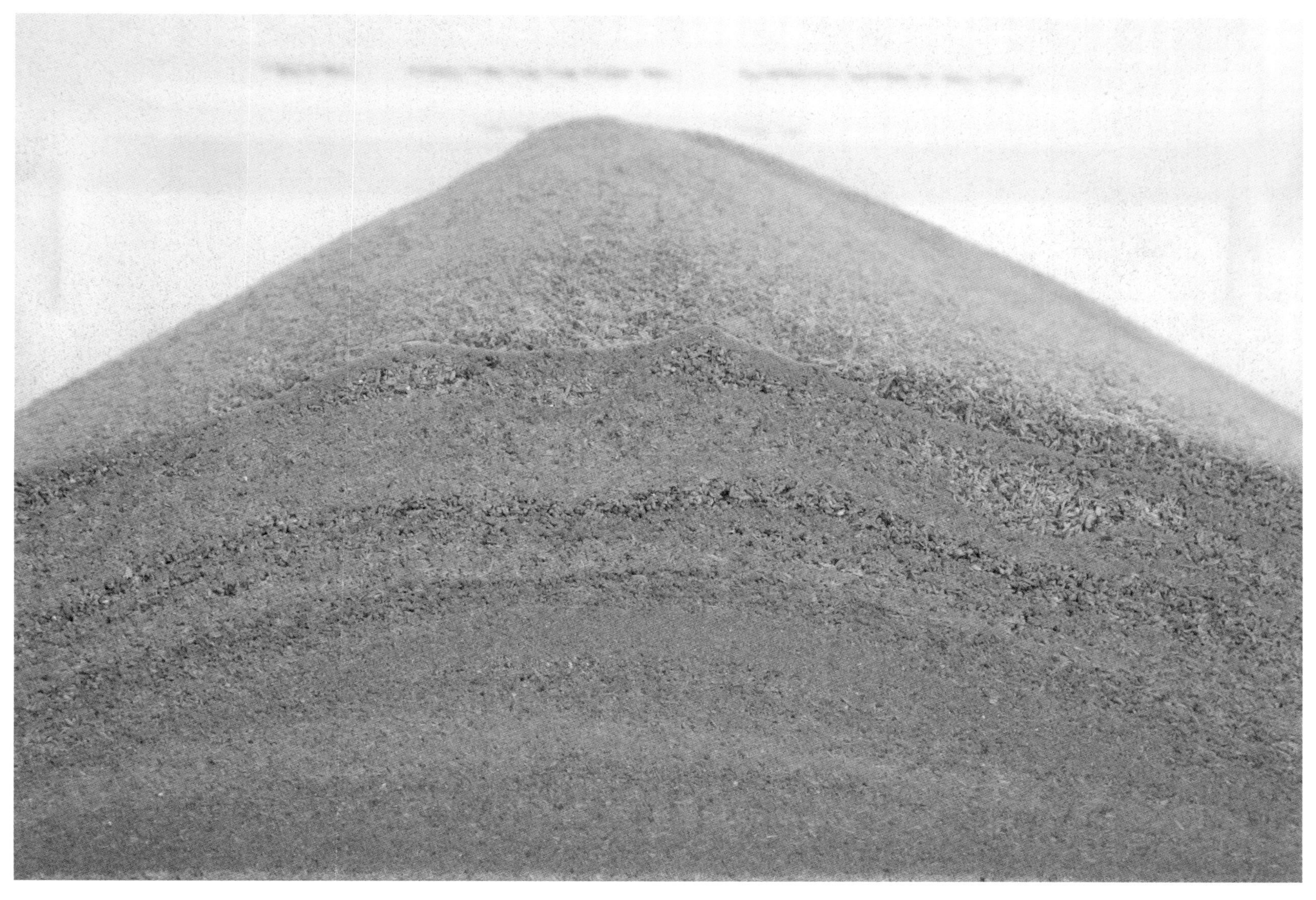

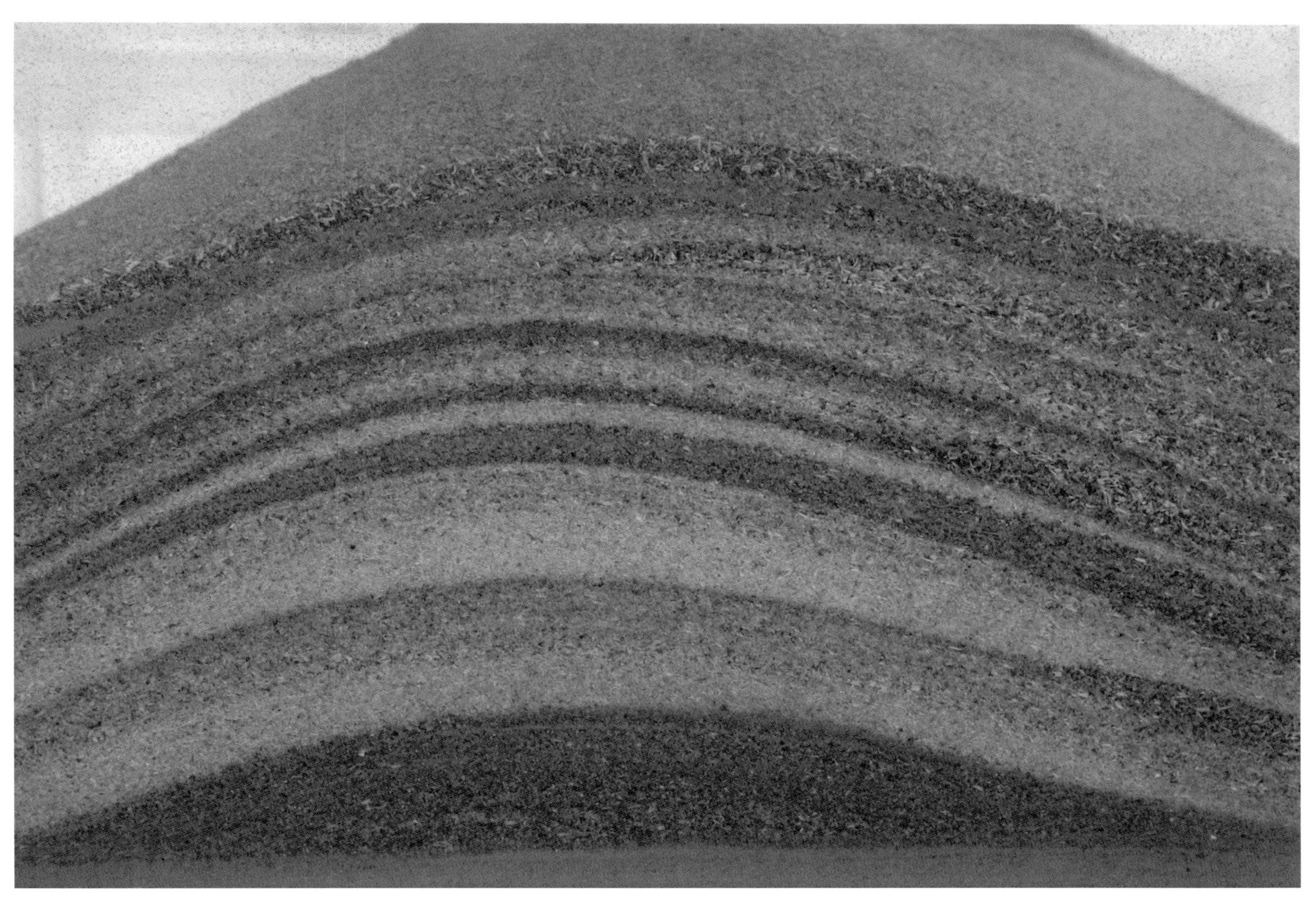

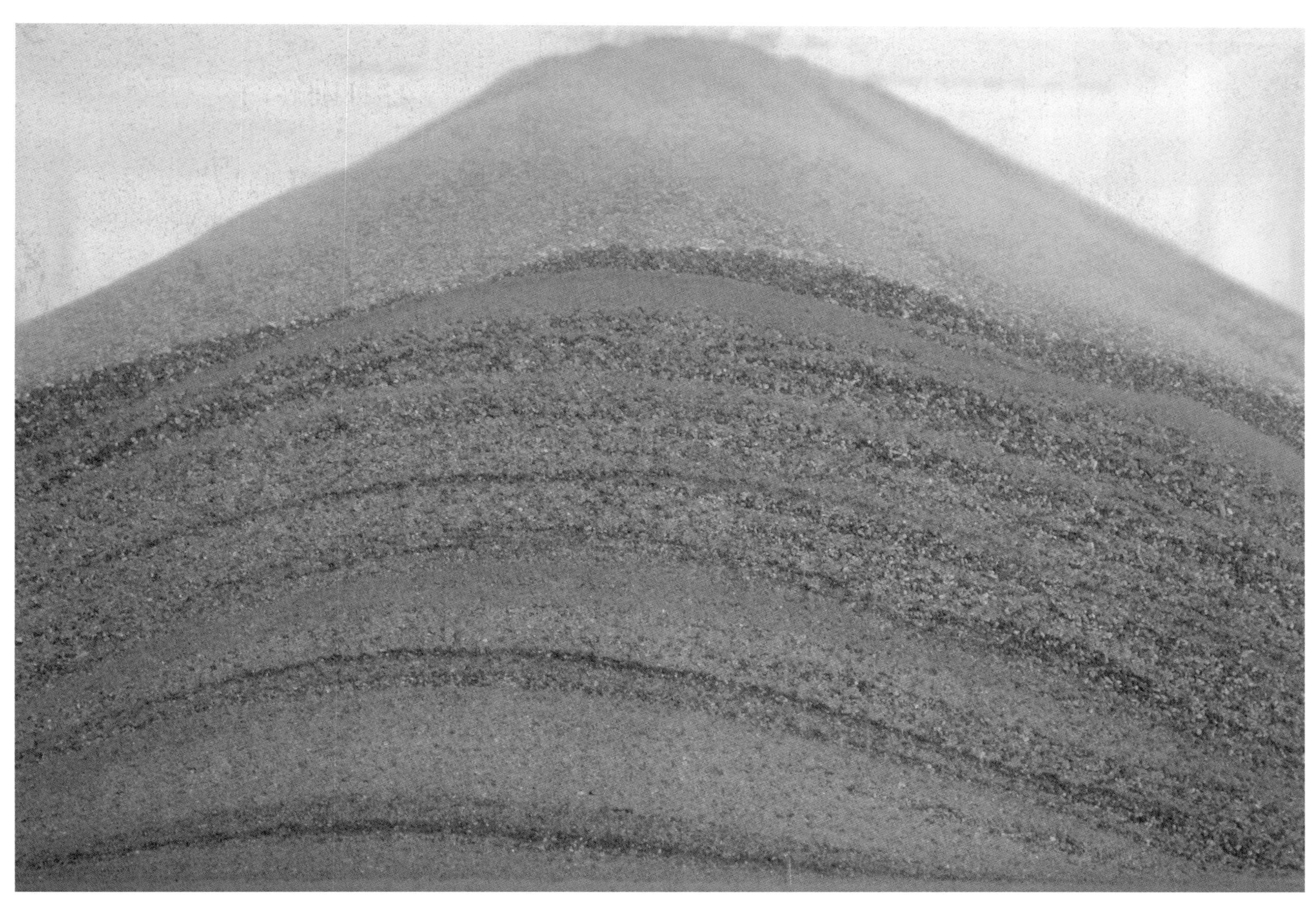

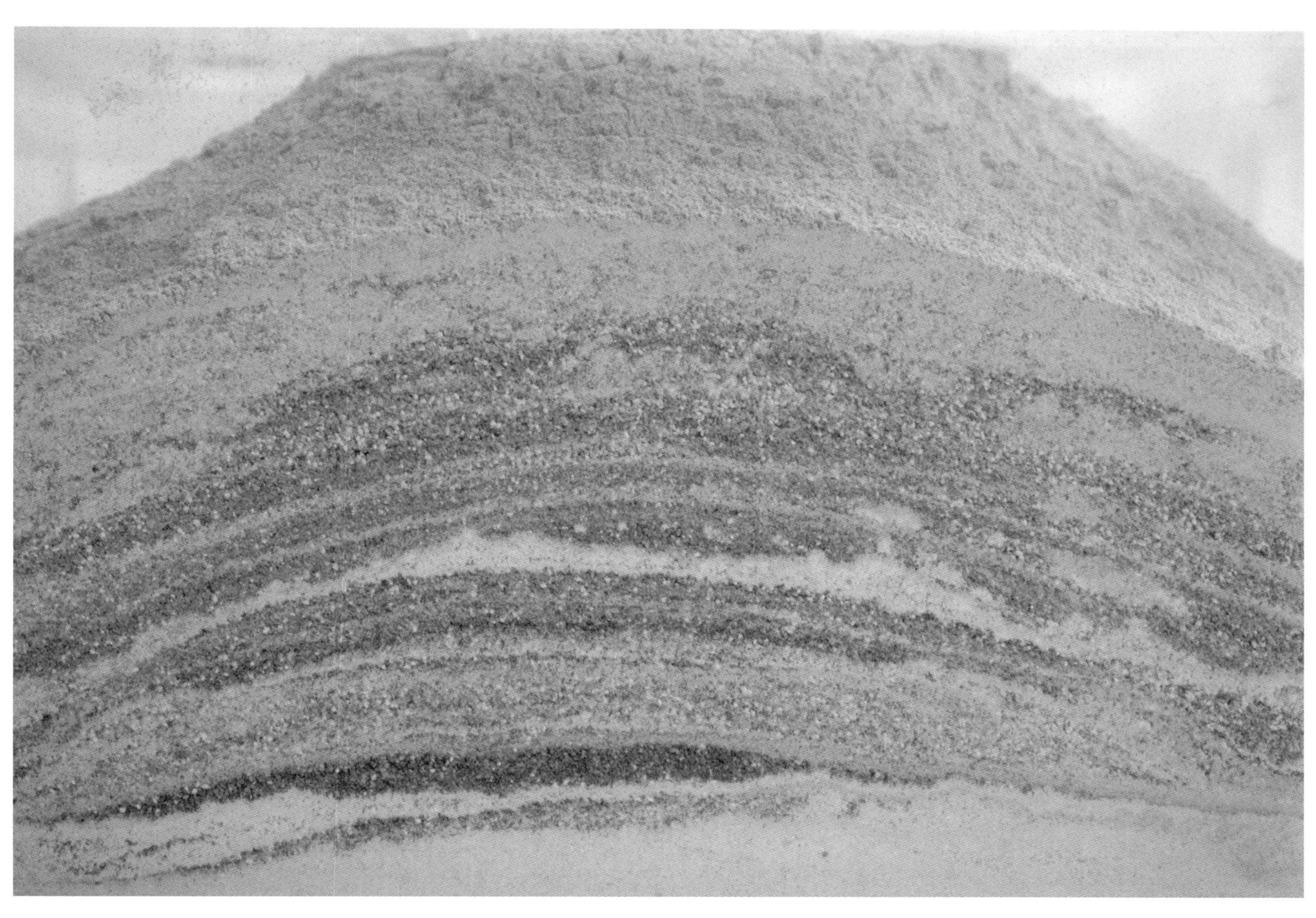

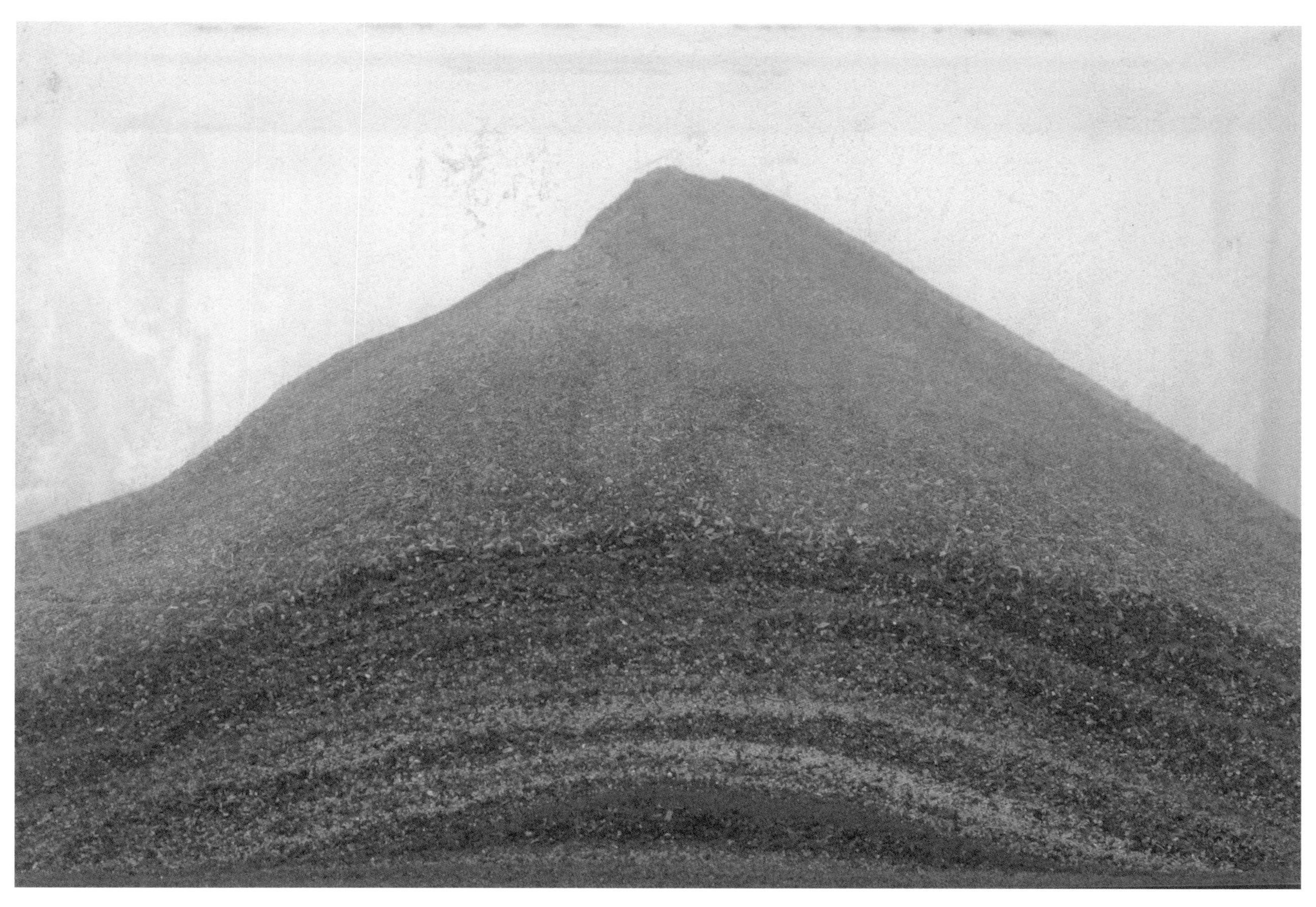

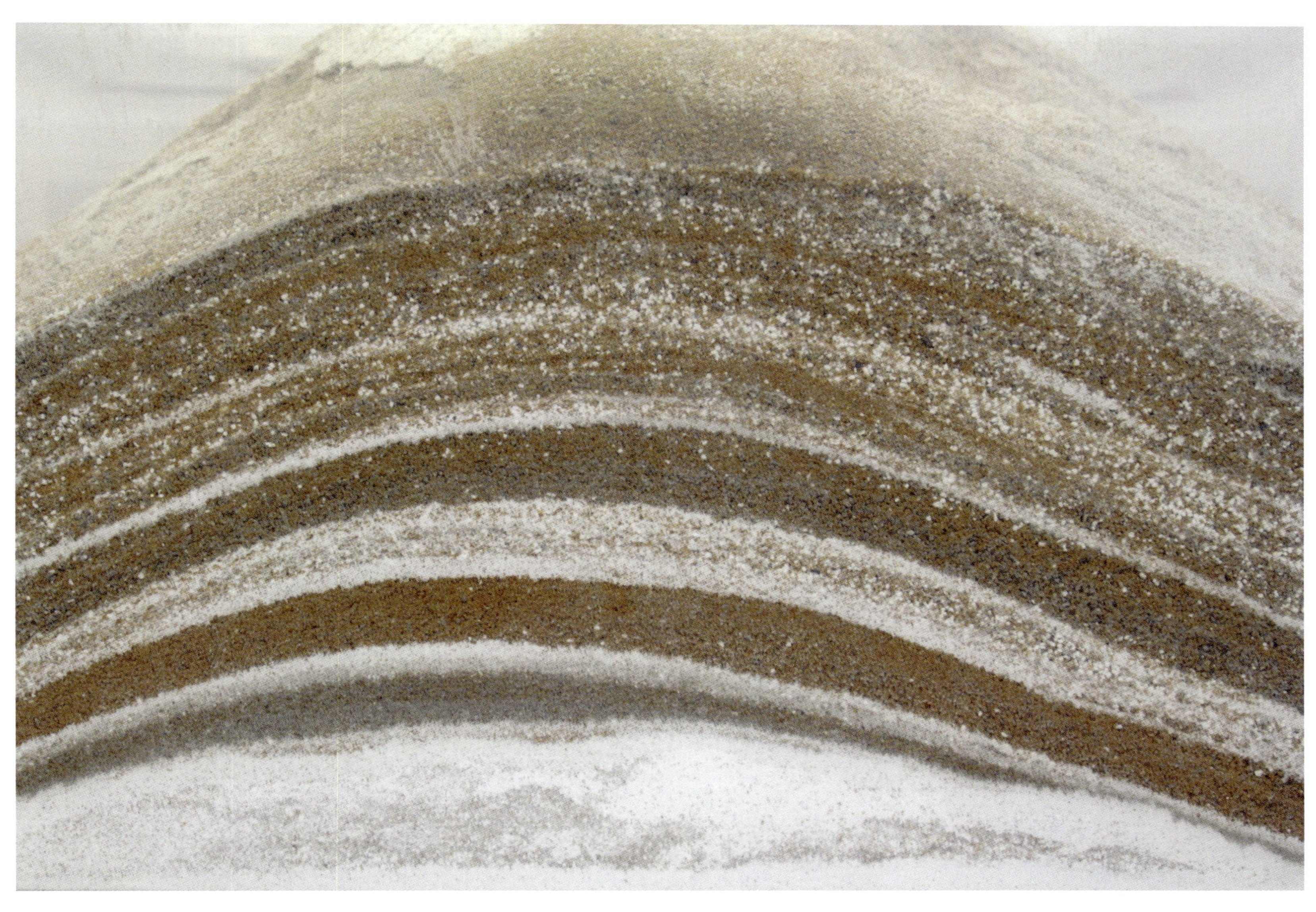

SAMPLED HISTORY

Once a month during the renovation of De Garage, Kris Van Dessel collected a sample of rubble from the site. In the period from March 2013 to December 2014, he took 22 samples in total, each of which he carefully filtered and meticulously stored in chronological order in his atelier, their temporary resting place. These were preserved in transparent containers, which started to form a stacked representation of muted earth colours showing the geological strata of the renovation's gradual progress. The resulting stack would not have looked out of place in an archaeological research facility. The artist's subtle presence amid all the activity of the construction site must have appeared quite inconspicuous. This tightly rhythmic series of actions manifests itself in the solo exhibition Sampled History, in which the artist has transposed the samples to the exhibition space in one simple, geo-artistic gesture. He mixes every sample of material with a specific amount of water and applies these emulsions to the walls of the exhibition space, employing a syntax of consecutive, chronological layers.

Sampling means borrowing a characteristic piece of another creation with the intention of incorporating it in one's own work. The principle was first observed in the mid-20th century in the French musical movement Musique Concrète, in which existing sounds were incorporated into sound collages. Something similar can be observed here in this context. Through the schematic, geological representation of the renovation process, the scars of former artistic productions are made visible in the epidermis of the exhibition space. The archaeology of cultural production in De Garage is gradually revealed by the artist. This intervention recalls a memory – albeit inverted – of Pierre Huyghe's intervention piece 'Timekeepers'. Here, the layer-after-layer exposure of erased presentations in the wall's paintwork makes way for Van Dessel's forensic detection of clues across the wall's surface. The carefully-applied pigments are expertly brushed away after a certain amount of drying time has allowed the added water to evaporate. Characteristic of Van Dessel's recent work is the recurring principle of completely returning the raw materials he has used in his artistic process to the earth. The substances are returned to their origin – like a field recording played back at the location where it was recorded.

The work of Kris Van Dessel is not to be categorised as a series of manufactured artefacts bound to or positioned in an exhibition space. His work would better be described as offering cross-sections of discoveries made tangible – the results of poetic-artistic research, presented here as food for thought for the observer. In addition to the renovation works that have fundamentally changed the architecture of the spaces, Kris Van Dessel has, with the utmost discretion, created a parallel space that breaks through the established time-space continuum. It's wonderful to get lost in his work, that is, once you've wormed your through the formal, syntactic trail of consecutive, chronological, two-dimensional layers; reaching the light at the end of the wormhole, you are free to reflect on what has been and what could be in the future of the safe haven that is art – now surely more essential than ever.

'(…) In other words, to perceive the whole is to leave the fragments displaced.' Robert Smithson

Beatrijs Eemans

APE#048
Kris Van Dessel, Sampled History

ISBN 9789490800307
www.artpapereditions.org
www.krisvandessel.be
First edition of 300 copies

The release of this book coincides with the exhibition 'Sampled History' at De Garage in Mechelen and organized by Cultuurcentrum Mechelen (16.01.2014 – 15.03.2014)
Text: Beatrijs Eemans
Translation: Jonathan Beaton
Graphic design: Studio Jurgen Maelfeyt
Printing: New Goff, Ghent
First print: January 2015

Special thanks to: Koen Leemans, Goele De Bruyn, Beatrijs Eemans, Diederik van der Mieden, Jurgen Maelfeyt, Dimitri Riemis and Charlotte Van Dessel

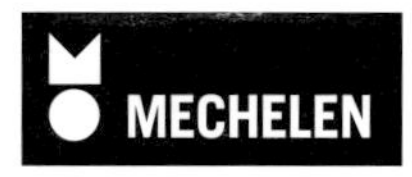

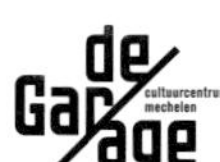

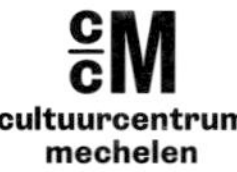